THE ENCYCLOPEDIA OF
WINDOW FASHIONS

700 decorating ideas for Windows, Bedding and Accessories.

P9-DMO-427

CHARLES T. RANDALL

ILLUSTRATED BY
Patricia Marovich Howard
Design Visuals
Fountain Valley, California

COVER DESIGN BY
Art Rojas
Rojas Design Inc.
Santa Ana, California

Published by

 RANDALL
INTERNATIONAL

Randall International
P.O. Box 1656
Orange, CA 92668 USA

The Publisher has made every effort to ensure that all instructions given in this book are accurate and safe but cannot accept liability for any resulting injury, damage or loss to either person or property whether direct or consequential and howsoever arising. The Publisher will be grateful for any information which will assist us in keeping future editions up to date.

ISBN 0-9624736-3-4

LC 91-090537

Copyright © 1992 by Charles T. Randall

Third Edition

All rights reserved. No part of this publication may be reproduced, stored in a retrieval system, or transmitted in any form or by any means, electronic, mechanical, photocopy, recording or otherwise, without the prior permission of the copyright owner.

Printed in the United States of America.

Contents

Glossary of Window Decorating Terms

A

"A" Frame Window — Very contemporary house structures sometimes forms an "A" shape. When draperies are used, they hang from the cross-beam of the "A," or they can be fabricated and installed to conform to the shape of the window.

Allowance — A customary variation from an "exact" measurement, taken for the purpose of anticipated needs.

Apron — A piece of wood trim beneath the window sill.

B

Bar-Tack — A sewing machine operation of repeated stitches concentrated to secure the lowest portion of drapery pleats.

Baton — A rod or wand used to hand draw traverse draperies.

Bay Window — A large projecting type of window made of a group of windows set at angles to each other and joined to each other on some sides.

Bottom Hem — The turned part forming a finished edge at bottom of drapery.

Bow Window — A large projecting type of window that is curved or semi-circular.

Box Pleat — A fold of cloth sewn into place to create fullness in a drapery. Box pleats are evenly spaced and stitched.

Bracket — Metal piece attached to the wall or casing to support a drapery or curtain rod.

C

Cafe — A traversing or non-traversing drapery, designed as a tier. The heading can be various styles. They can be set at a variety of heights to control ventilation, view and light.

Cafe Rod — A small, round decorative rod which comes in white, brass or woodgrain finish, used to mount cafe curtains that do not have a rod pocket. Cafe rods are meant to be seen and add an additional decorative touch to the curtain treatment.

Canopy — A fabric window topper created by sewing pockets into fabric panels and inserting a rod with a small projection at the top of the panel, a rod with a larger projection at the bottom.

Cantonniere — A three-sided shaped or straight cornice that "frames" the window — across the top and down the two sides. It is made of a hardboard, padded and covered with fabric.

Carriers — Small runners installed in a traverse rod which hold a drapery pin or hook.

Cartridge Pleat — A fold of cloth sewn into place to create fullness in a drapery. This is a round pleat 2-2½ inches in depth. Roundness is created by stuffing of crinoline or paper (removed for cleaning).

Cascade — A fall of fabric that descends in a zig-zag line from a drapery heading or top treatment.

Casement — (1) A cloth drapery that is of an open-weave material but more opaque than a sheer. (2) A type of vertically hinged window, whose panes open by sliding sideways or cranking outward.

Casing (Window) — Wooden frame around a window.

Center Draw — One pair of draperies which draws open and closes exactly at a window's center point.

Center Support — A metal grip which is used to support a traverse rod from above and prevents rod from sagging in the middle, but does not interfere with rod operation.

Clerestory Windows — A series of small windows which let in light and air. These are placed high on the wall to allow complete privacy.

Corner Window — A corner window literally wraps a corner of the building at right angles.

Cornice — A shallow, box-like structure, usually made of wood, fastened across the top of a window to conceal the drapery hardware.

Crinoline — A heavily sized, stiff fabric used as a foundation to support the edge of a hem or puffed sleeve. Also used as interlining.

Custom-Made Draperies — Draperies made to order in a workroom or decorator shop.

Cut Length — The cut length of the fabric is the length after allowances have been made for heading and hem.

D

Dormer Window — A dormer window is an upright window which breaks the surface of a sloping roof.

Double Hung — May be several items: Double hung window, Double hung shutters, and Double hung draperies (two sets of draperies usually sheer fabric under opaque fabric, both operating independently).

Draw Draperies — Panels of fabric, featuring pleated headings.

E

End Bracket — The two supporting metal grips which hold a drapery rod to the wall or ceiling. They control the amount of projection.

End Housing — Refers to the box parts at the extreme ends of a traverse drapery rod. They enclose the mechanism through which the cords run.

F

Fenestration — Location and proportion of windows in relationship to solid wall areas.

Festoon — A decorative drapery treatment of folded fabric that hangs in a graceful curve, and frames the top of a window.

Finial — Decorative end piece on cafe rods or decorative traverse rods (also referred to as "pole ends").

Finished Length — This is the length after draperies have been made, using the extra allowances in hem and heading.

French Pleats — This is a three-fold pleat and the one most often used in draperies.

H

Heading — The hemmed, usually stiffened, portion across the top of a curtain or drapery.

Hem — Refers to finished sides and bottom edges of a drapery.

Holdback — A decorative piece of hardware that holds draperies to each side of the window.

I

Insert Pulley — An auxiliary traverse rod part, over which the cords operate.

J

Jabot — A decorative vertical end of an over treatment that usually finishes a horizontal festoon.

Jamb — Interior sides of a door or window frame.

L

Lambrequin — A cornice that completely frames the window. Sometimes used interchangeably with valance or cantonniere.

Laminated Weights — Weight covered on both sides to avoid rust marks on drapery.

Lanai — A type of window covering made up of a series of hinged, rigid plastic panels, hung from a traverse track.

Lining — A fabric backing for a drapery.

Lintel — Lintels are wood, steel, or reinforced concrete beams placed over both window and door openings to hold up the wall and roof above.

M

Master Carrier — Two arms that overlap in center of rod when draperies are closed, allowing draperies to close completely.

Milium — Trade name for a thermal lining.

Mitered Corner — The formation of the bottom edge of drapery with a 45 degree angle on hem side.

Mullion — The vertical wood or masonry sections between a series of window frames.

Multi-Draw — A simultaneous opening and closing of several draperies on one rod at one time.

Muntin — The horizontal wood strips that separate panes of glass in windows.

O

Off-Center — A window not centered on a wall. Draperies still meet at its center point.

One-Way Draw — Drapery designed to draw one way only, in one panel.

Open Cuff — This is on the back side of drapery and at top. Open cuffs make one of the strongest type headings on any drapery. This results when you carry both fabrics to the top and make a turn with the crinoline.

Overlap — The overlap of a pair of draperies is that part of a drapery panel which rides the master carrier of a traverse rod and overlaps in the center when draperies are drawn closed. Usually 3½" on each side.

P

Panel — One half a pair of draperies or curtains.

Pattern Repeat — The "repeat" of a pattern is the distance between any given point in a design to where that exact point is repeated again.

Picture Window — A type of window with a large center glass area with usually two smaller glass areas on each side.

Pin-On-Hook — A metal pin to fasten draperies to a rod. It pins into drapery pleat and hooks to traverse carrier or cafe rod.

Pinch Pleats — A drapery heading where the basic pleat is divided into two or three smaller, equal pleats, sewn together at the bottom edge on the right side of the fabric.

Pleat — A fold of cloth sewn into place to create fullness.

Pleat To — "Pleat To" is the finished width of the fabric after it has been pleated. Example: A width of 48" fabric has been pleated to 18" — "Pleat To" 18".

Pleater Tape — Pocketed heading material designed to be used with pleating hooks.

Projection — Refers to a jutting out, an extension. On a curtain or drapery rod, it is that part which returns to the wall from the front of the rod.

Protractor — A drapery tool by which exact angles are measured (as in bay windows).

R

Ready-Mades — Standard size draperies, factory-made and available at local stores or through mail order sources.

Repeat — The space from one design motif to the next one on a patterned fabric.

Return — The distance from the face of the rod to the wall or casing where the bracket is attached.

Rod Pocket — A hollow sleeve in the top — and sometimes the bottom — of a curtain or drapery through which a rod is inserted. The rod is then attached to a solid wall surface.

S

Sash Curtain — Any sheer material hung close to the window glass. Usually hung from spring tension rods or sash rods mounted inside the window casing.

Sash Rod — A small rod, either decorative or plain, usually mounted inside a window frame on the sash.

Scalloped Heading — A popular top treatment for cafe curtains featuring semi-circular spaces between curtain rings.

Selvedge — The tightly woven edge on a width of fabric to hold the fabric together.

Side Hem — The turned part forming a finished edge at the side of the drapery.

Sill — The horizontal "ledge-like" portion of a window casing.

Slides — Small runners installed in a traverse rod which hold a drapery pin or hook.

Spacing — Refers to the flat space between pleats; the fuller the drapery, the less the spacing.

Stacking — The area required for draperies when they are completely opened.

Swag — A section of draped fabric above a window.

T

Tension Pulley — The pulley attachment through which the traverse cords move for one continuous smooth operation when drapery is drawn. May be mounted on baseboard, casing or wall, on one or both sides.

Tiebacks — Decorative pieces of hardware, sometimes called holdbacks. Available in many forms and designed to hold draperies back from the window to allow light passage or add an additional decorative touch to the window treatment.

Tier — Curtain layers arranged one above the other with a normal overlap of 4". Upper tiers project from the wall at a greater distance than lower panel to allow each curtain to hang free.

Traverse — To draw across. A traverse drapery is one that opens or closes across a window by means of the traverse rod from which it is hung.

U

Under-Draperies — A lightweight drapery, usually a sheer, closest to the window glass. It hangs beneath a heavier over-drapery.

V

Valance — A valance is a horizontal decorative fabric treatment used at the top of draperies to screen hardware and cords.

W

Weights — (chain and lead) Lead weights are sewn in at the vertical seams and each corner of drapery panel. Chain weights are small beads strung in a line along bottom hemline of sheers, to insure an even hemline and straight hanging.

Width — A word to describe a single width of fabric. Several widths of fabric are sewn together to make a panel of drapery. "Panel" is sometimes used in referring to a width of fabric.

Glossary of Fabrics and Fabric Terms

A

Antique Satin — One of the most common drapery fabrics sold. Characterized by a lustrous effect, normally composed of rayon/acetate blends.

B

Basketweave — Plain under-and-over weave; primarily in draperies.

Batiste — A soft finished fabric which has a high count of fine yarns. It is more opaque than voiles. Usually composed of 100% polyester or a polyester blend.

"Beta" Fiberglas Fiber — This filament is around .00010 inch in diameter, about one half the diameter of other glass fibers in use at present. Properties include improved flexibility, greater resistance to mechanical abuse to afford greater wearability, increased softness and suppleness and less irritation. "Beta" is used in apparel, home furnishings, and industrial fields. A registered trademark name of Owens-Corning Fiberglas Corp., N.Y.C.

Boucle — French for curled, indicates a curled or looped surface.

Brocade — Rich jacquard — woven fabric with all-over interwoven design of raised figures or flowers. Brocade has a raised surface in contrast to felt damask, and is generally made of silk, rayon and nylon yarns with or without metallic treatment.

Burlap — Coarse, canvas-like fabric made of jute, hemp or cotton. Also called Gunny.

C

Casements — Open weave casual fabric, characterized by its instability.

Challis — One of the softest fabrics made. Normally made of rayon and also combined with cotton.

Chintz — Glazed cotton fabric often printed with gay figures and large flower designs. Some glazes will wash out in laundering. The only durable glaze is a resin finish which will withstand washing or dry cleaning. Unglazed chintz is called cretonne.

Corduroy — A cut filling-pile cloth with narrow to wide wales which run in the warp direction of the goods and made possible by the use of an extra set of filling yarns in the construction. The back is of plain or twill weave, the latter affording the better construction. Washable types are available and stretch and durable press garments of corduroy are very popular. Usually an all-cotton cloth, some of the goods are now made with nylon or rayon pile effect on a cotton backing fabric or with polyester-cotton blends.

Crash — A coarse fabric having a rough irregular surface obtained by weavig thick uneven yarns. Usually cotton or linen, sometimes spun rayon or blends.

Crinoline — A heavily sized, stiff fabric used as a foundation to support the edge of a hem or puffed sleeve. Also used as interlining.

D

Damask — Firm, glossy jacquard-patterned fabric. Damask is similar to brocade, but flatter and reversible. It can be made from linen, cotton, rayon or silk, or a combination of fibers.

Double Knit — A fabric knitted with a double stitch on a double needle frame to provide a double thickness and is the same on both sides. It has excellent body and stability.

F

Faille — Plain weave (flat-rib); with filling yarns heavier than warp.

Foamback — Term used to denote that a fabric has been laminated to a backing of polyurethane foam.

G

Glasing — Thin finish provides luster, sheen, shine or polish to some fabrics. Chintz is an example of a glazed fabric.

H

Hand, Handle — The reaction of the sense of touch, when fabrics are held in the hand. There are many factors which give "character or individuality" to a material observed through handling. A correct judgement may thus be made concerning its capabilities in content, working properties, drapability, feel, elasticity, fineness and softness, launderability, etc.

I

Inherent Flame Frees — Fabric woven of flame-resistant fabric (not processed) and flame-free for life of the fabric.

L

Linen — This is a product of the flax plant. Among the properties of linen are rapid moisture absorption, no fuzziness, does not soil quickly, a natural luster and stiffness.

M

Matelasse — Appearance of a quilted weave; figured pattern with a raised, bubbly surface.

Modacrylic — A modified fiber in which the fiber-forming substance of any longchain synthetic polymer is composed of less than 85%, but at least 25% of weight of acrylonitrile units.

Mohair — Comes from the Angora goat, one of the oldest animals known to man. It is lighter weight drapery fabric; slightly brushed or hairy finish.

Moire — A finish given cotton, silk, acetate, rayon, nylon, etc., where bright and dim effects are observed. This is achieved by passing the fabric between engraved rollers which press the particular motif into the fabric.

N

Ninon — A smooth, transparent, high textured type of voile fabric. Usually made from 100% polyester.

O

Ombre — A graduate or shade effect of color used in a striped motif. Usually ranges from light to dark tones.

Organdy — Very light and thin, transparent, stiff and wiry cotton cloth. Will withstand repeated launderings and still retain its crispness. Organdy is a true, durable finish cloth.

Satin Weave — One of the three basic weaves, the others being plain weave and the twill weave. The surface of satin weave cloth is almost made up entirely of warp or filling floats since in the repeat of the weave, each yarn of the one system passes or floats over or under all but one yarn of the opposite yarn system. Satin weaves have a host of uses — brocade, brocatelle, damask other decorative materials.

Selvage — Each side edge of a woven fabric and an actual part of the warp in the goods. Other names for it are listing, self-edge, and raw edge.

Silk — The only natural fiber that comes in a filament form, reeled from the cocoon, cultivated or wild.

Slub Yarn — Yarn of any type which is irregular in diameter; may be caused by error, or purposely made with slubs to bring out some desired effect to enhance a material.

T

Taffeta — A fine plain weave fabric smooth on both sides, usually with a sheen on its surface.

Terry Cloth — This cloth fabric has uncut loops on both sides of the cloth. Terry is also made on a Jacquard loom to form interesting motifs.

Texture — The first meaning is the actual number of warp threads and filling picks per inch in any cloth that has been woven. Texture is also much used by the public and in advertising circles to mean the finish and appearance of cloth.

Thread Count — 1. The actual number of warp ends and filling picks per inch in a woven cloth. Texture is another name for this term. 2. In knitted fabric, thread count implies the number of wales or ribs, and the courses per inch.

V

Velour — 1. A term loosely applied to cut pile cloths in general; also to fabrics with a fine raised finish. 2. A cut pile cotton fabric comparable with cotton velvet, but with a greater and denser pile. 3. A staple, high grade woolen fabric which has a close, fine, dense, erect, and even nap which provides a soft, pleasing hand.

Velvet — A warp pile cloth in which a succession of rows of short cut pile stand so close together as to give an even, uniform surface. When the pile is more than one-eighth of an inch high, the cloth is usually called plus.

Voile — A thin open mesh cloth made by a variation of plain weave. Most voiles are made of polyester. Similar to ninon, but with a much finer denier of yarn with a very soft, drapable hand.

W

Warp — The yarns which run vertically or lengthwise in woven fabric.

Weft Yarn — The yarn runs horizontal or cross yarns.

Drapery Fabrics — Look & Performance

Satins and Jacquards
Usually the most formal and traditional, they are generally made from tightly woven, heavy, soft material which hangs straight from top to bottom in (formal) folds.

Casements, Open Weaves
These have a lighter, more casual feel. They are usually made from loosely woven, textured yarns that hang in looser folds than the formal satins and Jacquards.

Sheers
Made of soft, see-through fabrics, sheers are appropriate in most decors. Light and airy, they are sometimes used in combination with heavier draperies in more formal settings. They are billowy unless weighted, and can be made to drape quite well.

Prints
Suitable in most decors, prints are made from a light, tightly woven fabric, usually cotton or cotton-polyester blends.

Drapery Linings
Linings add substantially to the luxurious appearance necessary for good window treatments, and also provide a fuller pleated look for maintaining a soft drapable hand.

The lined-look provides uniformity to the exterior appearance of a home while allowing a broad choice of textures, weaves, colors and patterns for the interior.

The combination of sunlight and air pollution will eventually take its toll on all colors. There is no such thing as an absolutely colorfast material or dye. Some colors, however will show fading more dramatically than others. Bright colors tend to show fading more than subdued tones, and solids before prints.

Linings help draperies last longer. They afford some protection against sun and fading. They also protect the draperies from water stains — either from condensation on the inside of the window or from a sudden shower.

Insulated linings contribute to energy conservation, keeping homes cooler in summer and warmer in winter.

Textile Fibers & Their Properties

NATURAL FIBERS

COTTON

Drapability:	excellent hang, soft hand
Color fastness:	good, vat dyes best
Sun resistance:	excellent, does not sun rot
Abrasion resistance:	excellent
Sagging:	does not stretch, except when wet
Resiliency:	poor, packs easily, wrinkles easily, very absorbent, burns
Care:	wash or dry clean and iron at high temperature

Cotton generally wears excellently in drapery (print or plains).

LINEN OR FLAX

Drapability:	good hang, but not as soft as cotton
Color fastness:	good to poor, prints do not hold their color as well as plain fabrics
Sun resistance:	excellent, does not sun rot
Abrasion resistance:	excellent
Sagging:	strong, does not stretch
Resiliency:	poor, packs badly, does wrinkle
Care:	dry clean and iron at high temperature

Linens are excellent in plain and casement fabric and good in prints.

SILK

Drapability:	good hang, medium to soft hand
Color fastness:	good
Sun resistance:	poor, rots in short time, lining helps
Abrasion resistance:	good
Sagging:	strong, does not sag
Resiliency:	good, does not pack badly
Care:	dry clean and iron at medium temperature

Little silk is used in drapery today. This is due to sun rot and cost.

WOOL

There is virtually none used in drapery fabric.

MAN-MADE

RAYON

Drapability:	good hang, soft hand
Color fastness:	good to excellent (solution dyed)
Sun resistance:	good, but not as good as cotton or linen
Abrasion resistance:	good, but not as good as nylon or cotton
Sagging:	poor, stretches in loose yarns, but OK in tight woven fabrics
Resiliency:	good, does not pack, wrinkles less than cotton or linen
Care:	dry clean and iron at medium temperature

Rayon is blended with other fibers: cotton, acetate and linen.

ACETATE

Drapability:	good hand, soft hand
Color fastness:	good (solution dyed)
Sun resistance:	good, not as good as cotton and linen
Abrasion resistance:	good, but not as good as cotton or nylon
Sagging:	poor stretches in loose yarns, but OK in tight woven fabrics
Resiliency:	good, does not pack, wrinkles less than cotton or linen
Care:	dry clean and iron at low temperature

Blends well with other fibers, rayon and nylon.

POLYESTER

Drapability:	excellent hang, very soft hand
Color fastness:	good to excellent
Sun resistance:	excellent
Abrasion resistance:	good, sheers must be handled with care. Fabric can be bruised.
Sagging:	excellent, does not stretch or shrink
Resiliency:	good to excellent, does not pack, wrinkle free
Care:	wash or dry clean and iron at low temperature temperature

Polyester is an excellent fabric for most drapery applications. It blends well with other fibers. In polyester cotton blends, cotton wrinkles less.

NYLON

Drapability:	good, soft to stiff hand, not as soft as polyesters
Color fastness:	good to excellent
Sun resistance:	poor
Abrasion resistance:	excellent
Sagging:	excellent, does not sag
Resiliency:	excellent, does not pack, wrinkle free
Care:	dry clean and iron at low temperature

Nylon is not widely used in drapery fabric.

ACRYLIC

Drapability:	excellent, very soft hand
Color fastness:	excellent, if solution dyed
Sun resistance:	excellent, good as cotton or linen
Abrasion resistance:	good
Sagging:	very good, does not stretch
Resiliency:	very good, does not pack and wrinkle free
Care:	dry clean and iron at low temperature 50°

Acrylic fabrics hang well and do not sag. Can be blended with polyester. Modacrylics are flameproof.

DYNEL

Drapability:	excellent, soft hand like acrylic
Color fastness:	excellent
Sun resistance:	good to excellent
Abrasion resistance:	excellent
Sagging:	excellent compared to rayon or acetate
Resiliency:	very good, does not pack, wrinkle free, low flamability
Care:	Wash only, ironing does not affect it much, use low heat

Basic Window Types

1. **Double Hung Window** — Most common of all window types, has two sashes, one or both of which slide up and down. Unless it is too long and narrow or in the wrong location, this type of window is usually one of the easiest to decorate.

2. **In-Swinging Casement** — Opens into the room. If it is not decorated properly, curtains and draperies may tangle with the window as it is opened and closed.

3. **Out-Swinging Casement** — Opens outward. Both in-swinging and out-swinging casements may be operated by a crank, or simply moved by hand. Out-swinging casements are easily decorated.

4. **Ranch or Strip Windows** — Most often a wide window set high off the floor. Usually has sliding sashes and is common to most ranch type houses. It requires special consideration when decorating to make it attractive.

5. **Awning Window** — Has wide, horizontal sashes that open outward to any angle; can usually be left open when it's raining. Unless it is awkwardly placed or shaped, it's an easy one to decorate.

6. **Jalousie Window** — Identified by narrow, horizontal strips of glass that open by means of a crank to any desired angle. Decorating problems result only when the shape or location is unusual.

7. **Picture Window** — One designed to frame an outside view. It may consist of one large, fixed pane of glass, in which case the window cannot be opened. Or it may have movable sections on one or both sides of a fixed pane — or above and below — which can be opened for ventilation. Sometimes there are decorating problems, but in general, a picture window is your big opportunity.

8. **Dormer Window** — Usually a small window projecting from the house in an alcove-like extension of the room. It requires a treatment all its own.

9. **Bay Windows** — Three or more windows set at an angle to each other in a recessed area. You can use lots of imagination with bay windows.

11

10. **Bow Window** — A curved window, sometimes called a circular bay.

10.

11. **Slanting Window** — Often called "cathedral" window, usually an entire wall of the room. Its main characteristic is the angle at the top where the window follows the line of a slanting roof. This top slanting line often causes decorating concern, but the problem can be solved very effectively.

11.

12. **Double Windows** — Side by side windows. (If there are more than one they are often called multiple windows.) Most often treated as a single unit, always think of them together, as one decorating element.

12.

13. **Corner Windows** — Any window that comes together at the corner of a room.

13.

14. **French Doors** — Sometimes called French windows. They come in pairs and often open onto a porch or patio. Usually they need special decorating to look their best.

14.

15. **Sliding Glass Doors** — Today's functional version of French doors. They are often set into a regular wall, but are sometimes part of a modern "glass wall." Either way, they need special decor that allows them to serve as doors yet provide nighttime privacy.

15.

16. **Clerestory Window** — A shallow window set near the ceiling. Usually should be decorated inconspicuously. (In modern architecture, it is sometimes placed in the slope of a beamed ceiling, in which case it should rarely be decorated at all.)

16.

17. **Palladian Window** — An arched top window with straight panes below the arch.

17.

18 **Glass Wall** — Usually a group of basic window units made to fit together, forming a veritable "wall" of windows. Curtains and draperies often require special planning.

18.

WINDOWS WITH A CHALLENGE

Door with Window & Sidelights

SOLUTION 1

SOLUTION 2

Corner Gliding Windows with Structural Beam on Top

SOLUTION 1

SOLUTION 2

13

Corner Windows

SOLUTION 1

SOLUTION 2

SOLUTION 3

SOLUTION 4

SOLUTION 5

**Air Conditioner in a
Double-Hung Window**

SOLUTION 1

SOLUTION 2

**Sliding Glass Doors &
Cathedral Windows**

SOLUTION 1

SOLUTION 2

15

SOLUTION 3

SOLUTION 4

SOLUTION 5

SOLUTION 6

Clerestory Windows

SOLUTION 1

Bay with Casement Windows

SOLUTION 1

SOLUTION 2

SOLUTION 3

Picture Window with Baseboard Heater

SOLUTION 1

SOLUTION 2

SOLUTION 3

Jalousie Windows & Doors

SOLUTION 1

SOLUTION 2

SOLUTION 3

French Doors

SOLUTION 1

SOLUTION 2

SOLUTION 3

18

Triple Double-Hung Windows

SOLUTION 1

SOLUTION 2

SOLUTION 3

Bay with Double-Hung Windows

SOLUTION 1

SOLUTION 2

SOLUTION 3

SOLUTION 2

SOLUTION 3

SOLUTION 4

SOLUTION 5

Scarf Swag Held by Rosettes over
Draperies Gathered on Wide Rod

Triple Swags over Tie-backs

French Pleated Tie-backs on Arched Rod

Stationary Draperies gathered on rod
Curved Sleeve-Valance with Bows

Puffed Tie-back Drapery
on Arched Rod. Pleated
Shade Under.

Double Rod Pocket Drapery
with High Tie-backs. Woven
Wood Under.

Arched Bishop Sleeve Draperies
over Balloon Shade

Knotted Lace Swag
over Lace Draperies

Arched Gathered Valance over Draperies

Single Swag with Rosette over Draperies

25

Tabbed Draperies with Valance
on Dec Rod

Gathered Draperies with Sleeve
on Dec Rod

Draperies on Dec Rod with
Special Swag Effect

Draperies on Dec Rod

Gathered Valance over Bishop
Sleeve Draperies with Cafe Curtain

Single Swag over Draperies
and Cafe Curtain

Sheer Valance over Tie Backs

Gathered Valance over Draperies

27

Gathered Valance over Tie Backs

Gathered and Swagged Valance over Tie Backs

Gathered Valance with Draperies with Draperies Pulled Back

Double Arched Valance over Tie Backs + Cloud Valance

Pleated Arched Valance over
Tie Backs and Sheer Balloon

Gathered Top Arched Valance
over Bow Tie Backs

Double Gathered Valance with
Brass Rod in Middle over Blind

Single Tabbed Drapery with
Bows and Tie Back Holder

29

Tabbed Drapery Tied Back on One Side

Pleated Draperies Tied Back

Pleated Tie Back Draperies on Dec Rod

Double Gathered R & B Valances over Tie Backs

Alternate Heading Styles

Rod Pocket Drapery with Center Sleeve & Tie-backs

Double Flat Rod Tie-backs with Heading

Bishop Sleeve Draperies with Valance

Arched Valance with Ruffle & Ruffled
Tie-backs over Cafe Curtains

Tie-back Draperies with Balloon Valance

Tied-back Draperies with Accent Band –
Shirred Valance

Tie-backs with Ruffle at top –
Sheers under·

Wide Rod Pocket Drapery Tied Back

Rod Pocket Drapery over Cafe RTD

Rod Pocket Tie-backs with Ruffles

Rod Pocket Valance with Rod Pocket Cafe

Rod Top & Bottom Valance with matching
Shirred Tie-bands – Mini Blind

Tied-back Draperies with Continental Top
Matching Cafe Curtain under

Triple Tie-backs on Continental Rod with Stand-up Top

CONTINENTAL™ is a registered trademark of Kirsch-Cooper Industries.

Rod Top Draperies with Center Florence
& low Tie-backs over Mini Blind

Draperies gathered on Dec. Pole
over Austrian Shade

Rod Top Draperies with Multiple Bow Ties over Roman Shade

Multiple Tie Back Draperies

Tie-back Draperies with Austrian
Valance & Shade

Space pleated Queen Ann Valance with
scalloped edge over Tie-backs & Sheers

40

Multiple Tie-backs over Cafe Curtains for a warm Country feeling

Pinch Pleated Drapery with Fringe

Ruffled Tie-backs with Bow & Rosettes
over Pull-down Shade

Rod Top Only Balloon Draperies

Double Rod Top Valance with
Puffed Tie-backs over Sheers

End-pleated Valance with Puffed
Tie-backs over Lace Curtain

42

Custom Made Draperies

Standard Workmanship and Quality Features

- Double Heading
- 4" Permanent Buckram Headings
- Pleating custom tacked with extra thread
- All seams serged and overlocked
- All draperies perfectly matched
- All draperies table sized
- Blind stitched bottom and side hems
- Double 4" bottom hems + 1½" Double side hems
- All draperies weighted at corners and seams.
- Multiple width draperies are pleated so that joining seams are hidden behind pleats.

Made to Custom Measurements

To any exact width or length.
Pleated to any desired fullness up to 3 to 1.
Lined or unlined.

Drapery Terminology

- Width is one strip of material (can be any length) which can be pleated to a finished dimension across the TOP of between 16" and 24". Using a 48" wide material as our base, a width of which finishes to 24" is considered double fullness or 2 to 1; 16" finished width is considered triple fullness or 3 to 1. Any number of widths can be joined together to make the draperies properly cover the window area.
- Panel is a single unit of drapery of one or more widths, which is used specifically for one way draw — stack left or stack right — and/or stationary units.
- Pair is two equal panels which are pleated to cover a desired area.
- Return is the measurement from the rod to the wall; in other words the projection.
- Overlap is the measurement, when draperies are fully closed, of having the right panel overlap the left panel. This is usually 3" for each panel. *Remember your customer must add 12" to the rod measurement to insure proper returns and overlaps.*

Options Available on Draperies

A variety of Headings:
Pinch Pleated with 4" buckram
Pinch Pleated with 5" buckram
Box Pleated
Box Pleated with Tabs for rod. Add diameter of rod to finished length. For flat tab draperies use 2-1.
Rod Pocket for shirred draperies.
Draperies may be self-lined, or
Draperies may be lined with black-out lining.

Pleat Spacing

Pleat spacings vary according to the widths of material used to achieve a specified finished width. For example: 3 widths of material pleated to 59 inches to the pair will not have the same pleat spacing as 3 widths of material pleated to 72 inches to the pair. If pleats and pleat spacing are to look alike on draperies of different widths, please specify "comparable fullness" on your order. *Vertically striped fabrics will not fabricate to allow an identical stripe to fall between each pleat, panel to panel, or pair to pair.*

How to Order Your Draperies

Since "Made-to-Measure" draperies are made to your exact specifications it is imperative that measurements be made with the greatest of care. We recommend that you double check all measurements for accuracy. All measuring should be done with a steel tape or yardstick. Measure each window separately even when they appear to be the same size. If length varies use dimension of shortest length.

Drapery Width

- Measure width of drapery rod from end to end.
- Add to this figure an extra 12" to include the allowance for standard traverse rod returns and overlap.
- Standard returns are 3" in depth. For over-draperies allow for clearance of under-curtain. A 6" return should be sufficient.
- When ordering panels that stack (draw) in one direction only, specify if the drapery is to stack (draw) left or right.

Drapery Length

- Measure from top of rod, to floor or to carpet. (By inserting pins 1" from top drapery will automatically clear the floor or carpet.)
- Under-curtain should be at least ½" shorter than over-drapery.
- When floor length draperies are used it is best to measure length at each side and in the center. Use shortest figure for your measurement.
- Rod should be placed a minimum of 4" above the window so hooks and pleats will not be observed from outside.
- If sill length, allow 4" below sill so bottom hem will not be observed from outside.
- When using pole rings, measure length from bottom of rings.

Caution: When both under-curtain and over-drapery are used, be sure to allow for clearance of face drapery. For example, an under-curtain with a 3½" return requires at least a 6" return on the over-drapery.

YARDAGE CHART FOR 4" OR 5" HEADING (Cut Plus 20")
TOTAL NUMBER OF WIDTHS PER PAIR OR PANEL

FINISHED LENGTH	2W	3W	4W	5W	6W	7W	8W	9W	10W	11W	12W	13W	14W	15W
36"	3¼	4¾	6¼	7¾	9¼	10¾	12¼	13¾	15¼	16¾	18¼	19¾	21¼	22¾
40"	3½	5	6½	8	9½	11	12½	14	15½	17	18½	20	21½	23
44"	3¾	5½	7¼	9	10¾	12½	14¼	16	17¾	19½	21¼	23	24¾	26½
48"	4	5¾	7½	9¼	11	12¾	14½	16¼	18	19¾	21½	23¼	25	26¾
52"	4	6	8	10	12	14	16	18	20	22	24	26	28	30
56"	4¼	6½	8½	10¾	12¾	15	16¾	19	21¼	23¼	25½	27½	29¾	31¾
60"	4½	6¾	9	11¼	13½	15¾	18	20	22¼	24½	26¾	29	31¼	33½
64"	4¾	7	9½	11¾	14	16½	18¾	21	23½	25¾	28	30½	32¾	35
68"	5	7½	10	12¼	14¾	17¼	19¾	22	24½	27	29½	32	34¼	36¾
72"	5¼	7¾	10¼	13	15½	18	20½	23	25¾	28¼	30¾	33¼	36	38½
76"	5½	8	10¾	13½	16	18¾	21½	24	26¾	29½	32	34¾	37½	40
80"	5¾	8½	11¼	14	16¾	19½	22¼	25	28	30¾	33½	36¼	39	41¾
84"	6	8¾	11¾	14½	17½	20¼	23¼	26	29	32	34¾	37¾	40½	43½
88"	6	9	12	15	18	21	24	27	30	33	36	39	42	45
92"	6¼	9½	12½	15¾	18¾	22	25	28	31¼	34¼	37½	40½	43¾	46¾
96"	6½	9¾	13	16¼	19¼	22¾	26	29	32¼	35½	38¾	42	45¼	48½
100"	6¾	10	13½	16¾	20	23½	26¾	30	33½	36¾	40	43½	46¾	50
104"	7	10½	14	17¼	20¾	24¼	27¾	31	34½	38	41½	45	48¼	51¾
108"	7¼	10¾	14¼	18	21½	25	28½	32	35¾	39¼	42¾	46¼	50	53½

RTB .... Cut Plus 12"   TIE BACKS .... CUT 12"

"ARDAGE CHART FOR 5" HEADINGS (DOUBLE) ... PLAIN FABRICS ONLY. CUT PLUS 20".

STACK BACK CHART

IF THE GLASS IS	TOTAL STACK-BACK SHOULD BE	ROD LENGTH AND DRAPERY COVERAGE SHOULD BE
38 inches	26 inches	64 inches
44	28	72
50	30	80
56	32	88
62	34	96
68	36	104
75	37	112
81	39	120
87	41	128
94	42	136
100	44	144
106	46	152
112	48	160
119	49	168
125	51	176
131	53	184
137	55	192
144	56	200
150	58	208
156	60	216
162	62	224
169	63	232
175	65	240
181	67	248
187	69	255

NOTE: You will have to ADD RETURNS AND OVERLAPS TO DRAPERY COVERAGE.

THIS CHART IS BASED ON AVERAGE PLEATING AND MEDIUM WEIGHT FABRIC. YOU MAY DEDUCT 7" FROM ROD LENGTH IF YOU ARE USING A ONE WAY ROD. IF BULKY FABRIC IS USED, ADD TO STACK-BACK ACCORDINGLY.

PLEAT-TO / FULLNESS CHARTS

(48" Fabric) 2½ X's Fullness

PLEAT-TO	19	38	57	76	95	114	133	152	171	190	209	228	247	266	285
WIDTHS	1	2	3	4	5	6	7	8	9	10	11	12	13	14	15

(48" Fabric) 3 X's Fullness

PLEAT-TO	15	30	45	60	75	90	105	120	135	150	165	180	195	210	225
WIDTHS	1	2	3	4	5	6	7	8	9	10	11	12	13	14	15

(54" Fabric) 2½ X's Fullness

PLEAT-TO	21	42	63	84	105	126	147	168	189	210	231	254	273	294	315
WIDTHS	1	2	3	4	5	6	7	8	9	10	11	12	13	14	15

(54" Fabric) 3 X's Fullness

PLEAT-TO	17	34	51	68	85	102	119	136	153	170	187	204	221	238	255
WIDTHS	1	2	3	4	5	6	7	8	9	10	11	12	13	14	15

FULLNESS CHART

48" Fabric	Pleated to 2½ X's fullness = 19" Panels
54" Fabric	Pleated to 2½ X's fullness = 21" Panels
60" Fabric	Pleated to 2½ X's fullness = 23" Panels

48" Fabric	Pleated to 3 X's fullness = 15" Panels
54" Fabric	Pleated to 3 X's fullness = 17" Panels
60" Fabric	Pleated to 3 X's fullness = 19" Panels

48" Fabric	Pleated to 2 X's fullness = 23" Panels
54" Fabric	Pleated to 2 X's fullness = 26" Panels
60" Fabric	Pleated to 2 X's fullness = 29" Panels

PLEAT TO CHART

Heavy Duty Rods

Oneway 3½" return add 5 inches
Center Open 3½ return add 12 inches

One Way 6" return add 7 inches
Center Open 6" return add 16 inches

Decorator Type Rods

One Way 3½" return add 7 inches
Center Open 3½" add 16 inches

One Way 6" return add 9 inches
Center Open 6" return add 19 inches

Arched Valance with Bows
Gathered on Rod

Cloud Valance with Stand-up Ruffle

Empire Valance with Jabots

Plain Banded Valance with Jabots

Tab-top Valance on Dec. Rod

Multiple Arched Valance Shirred on Rod

Rolled Stagecoach Valance
with Wide Knotted Tie Bands

Swags & Jabots over Plain Valance

Arched Valance with Top Ruffle

Gathered Valance on Top & Bottom Rods
with Multiple Bow Ties

Multiple Point Valance with Edge Banding

Box Pleated Valance with Twisted Cording

Triple Cone Pleated Valance on Dec Rod

Tapered Box Pleated Valance with Banding

Valance with Triple Box Pleats

Two Gathered Valances on Flat Rods
with Dec Rod in Middle

Gathered Valance on Flat Rod
with Dec Rods at Top & Bottom

Gathered Valance with Flat Rod in Middle
& Two Dec Rods Between

Two 4½" Flat Rods with Dec Rod in Middle

Two 4½" Flat Rods with
Dec Rods Top & Bottom

V102

Double Pinch Pleat

V101

Pleated Arched Valance

V100

French Pleated Valance

V103

Double Pleat Queen Ann

V104

Space Pleated Valance

V105

Queen Ann Valance

V137

Kingston Valance

V138

Space Pleated Queen Ann Valance

V108

RTO Arched Valance

V109

RTO Valance

V110

RTB Valance

V111

Double RTB Valance

V112

Double RTB Valance

V113

RTB Valance with Lower Rod Lifted

V114

Cloud Valance with Shirred Heading

V115

Cloud Valance with Rod Pocket Heading

V116

Cloud Valance with Stand-up Ruffle

V117

Balloon Valance with Welting

V118

Rod Top Swag & Cascade

V119

RTO Tapered Valance

V120

RTO Swag & Jabot Valance

V121

Austrian with Fringe

V122

Austrian with Jabots

V123

Austrian Valance with Cascades

Stagecoach Valance

Mock Roman

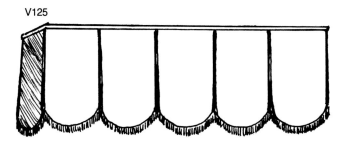

Scalloped Valance with Fringed Edge

Inverted Box Pleat

Inverted Box Pleat with Banding

Box Pleat with Banding

V130

Rod Pocket with Standup Ruffle

V129

Arched Rod Pocket

V141

Double Rod Pocket with
Standup Top & Bottom

V131

Double Rod Pocket with Standup

V142

Double Ruffled Valance Shirred on Rod

V132

Double Rod Pocket RTB with Standup

Rod Pocket Heading with No Standup

Double Rod Pocket with No Standup

Double Rod Pocket Balloon Valance

Triple Rod Pocket with Multiple Fabrics

4″ Shirred Heading

Arched 4″ Shirred Heading

V145

Shirred Double Arched Valance with Spaced Pleats

V146

Arched Spacer Valance

V147

Double Rod Pocket with Ruffles
& Tapered Sides

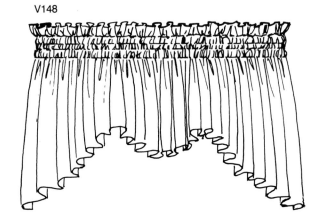

V148

Double Arched Valance with Shirred
Heading & Tapered Sides

V149

Shirred Cloud Valance with Dropped Sides & Ruffle

French Pleated Valance

Austrian Valance With
Side Cascades

Shirred 3-Tiered
Petticoat Valance

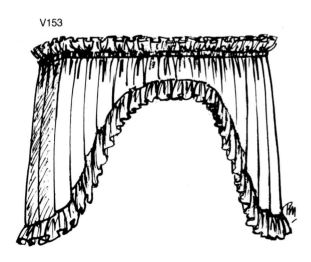

New Orleans Valance
With 6" Ruffle

Rod Pocket Valance
With Tapered Sides

YARDAGE INFORMATION

GENERAL TERMS

PLEAT-TO: Rod or Board facing plus returns.

FINISHED LENGTH: Length after fabrication. That is, the length you want the valance to be after the workroom makes it.

CUT LENGTH: Is the length of material figured per width consisting of the finished length plus the number of inches your workroom requires for heading, bottom hem, possible repeat, and allowance for trim off.

WIDTHS: Each piece of drapery fabric sewn together to form a pair or panel of draperies is a width. Example, a one way panel of draperies with a pleat-to of 110'' requires 6 widths of 48'' fabric. See fullness chart.

FULLNESS: The more fabric you pleat-to, or gather together to fill a given space. Usually two, two and a half, or three times fullness.

REPEAT: How many inches a pattern takes to repeat itself.

PLEAT-TO / FULLNESS CHARTS

(48'' Fabric) 2½ X's Fullness

PLEAT-TO	19	38	57	76	95	114	133	152	171	190	209	228	247	266	285
WIDTHS	1	2	3	4	5	6	7	8	9	10	11	12	13	14	15

(48'' Fabric) 3 X's Fullness

PLEAT-TO	15	30	45	60	75	90	105	120	135	150	165	180	195	210	225
WIDTHS	1	2	3	4	5	6	7	8	9	10	11	12	13	14	15

(54'' Fabric) 2½ X's Fullness

PLEAT-TO	21	42	63	84	105	126	147	168	189	210	231	254	273	294	315
WIDTHS	1	2	3	4	5	6	7	8	9	10	11	12	13	14	15

(54'' Fabric) 3 X's Fullness

PLEAT-TO	17	34	51	68	85	102	119	136	153	170	187	204	221	238	255
WIDTHS	1	2	3	4	5	6	7	8	9	10	11	12	13	14	15

YARDAGE REQUIREMENTS

V100, V101, V102, V103, V104, V105, V106, V107, V108, V109, V129, V130, V133, V135, V136, V137, V141, V142, V143, V144, V145, V146, V148.

For these valances determine widths required and fullness using fullness charts above. Gathered style valances usually look better with 300 percent fullness.

SELF LINED PLAIN FABRIC (recommended fullness 2½ - 3 X's)

Double finished length plus 10'' equals cut length. Cut length X's widths required divided by 36 equals yardage.

PLAIN FABRIC WITH LINING

Finished length plus 10'' X's required widths divided by 36 equals yardage. If you use lining for valance styles V101, V103, V105, V106, and V107 the lining may show from certain angles. For this reason, I feel its best to self-line these valances.

PRINTED FABRICS WITH LINING (lining recommended)

Finished length plus 10'' divided by repeat, rounded to higher whole number (if number is fractional). Whole number X's repeat equals cut length. Cut length X's widths needed divided by 36 equals yardage. Its better to use lining for print. This is because the print may bleed through in the light if self-lined.

V110, V111, V131, V134,

Determine widths required using fullness charts. Gathered style valances usually look better with 300 percent fullness.

SELF LINED PLAIN FABRIC

Double finished length plus 14'' equals cut length. Cut length X's widths divided by 36 equals yardage.

PLAIN FABRIC WITH LINING

Finished length plus 14'' equals cut lenght. Cut length X's widths divided by 36 equals yardage.

PRINTED FABRICS WITH LINING (lining recommended)

Finished length plus 16'' divided by repeat, rounded to higher whole number (if number is fractional). Whole number X's repeat equals cut length. Cut length X's widths required divided by 36 equals yardage.

V112,

Determine widths required using fullness charts. Gathered style valances usually look better with 300 percent fullness.

PLAIN FABRIC UNLINED OR LINED (self-lined not recommended)

Finished length plus 32'' equals cut length. Widths required X's cut length divided by 36 equals yardage. The extra length is needed because the installer lifts the lower rods to give the valance a cloud like look.

PRINTED FABRICS WITH LINING (recommended)

Finished length plus 30'' divided by repeat, then rounded to higher whole number (if number is fractional). Whole number X's repeat equals cut length. Cut length X's widths required divided by 36 equals yardage. The extra length is needed because the installer lifts the lower rods to give the valance a cloud like look.

V113,

PLAIN FABRIC UNLINED OR LINED

Finished length plus 24'' equals cut length. Widths required X's cut length divided by 36 equals yardage.

PRINTED FABRICS WITH LINING (recommended)

Finished length plus 22'' divided by repeat, then rounded to higher whole number (if number is fractional). Whole number X's repeat equals cut length. Cut length X's widths required divided by 36 equals yardage.

V114, V116, V117.

PLAIN FABRIC WITH LINING (lining recommended)

Finished length plus 20'' equals cut length. Pleat-to X's 3 divided by fabric width, then round to next whole width. This equals number of widths required. Widths required X's cut length divided by 36 equals yardage.

PRINTED FABRICS WITH LINING (recommended)

Finished length plus 20'' divided by repeat, then rounded to higher whole number (if number is fractional). Whole number X's repeat equals cut length. Pleat-to X's 3 divided by fabric width, then rounded to next whole width. This equals number of widths required. Widths required X's cut length divided by 36 equals yardage.

V115, V149

PLAIN FABRIC WITH LINING (lining recommended)

Finished length plus 30'' equals cut length. Pleat-to X's 3 divided by fabric width, rounded to next whole width. This equals widths required. Widths required X's cut length divided by 36 equals yardage.

PRINTED FABRICS WITH LINING

Finished length plus 30'' divided by repeat, then rounded to higher whole number (if number is fractional). Whole number X's repeat equals cut length. Pleat-to X's 3 divided by fabric width, rounded to next whole width. This equals width required. Widths required X's cut length divided by 36 equals yardage.

V118, V119, V120, V150, V151, V152, V153, V154

These are beautiful valances, but difficult to make. Not all workrooms can do them. If your workroom can do them, its best to have your workroom also figure out the yardage requirements.

V121, V122, V123,

PLAIN FABRIC UNLINED (recommended)

Finished length X's 3 equals cut length. Pleat-to X's two and a half, divided by fabric width, rounded to next whole width equals widths required. Widths required X's cut length divided by 36 equals yardage. For V123 add one extra yard every 5 feet for jabots, and add 3 yards extra for each cascade. For valance V123 cascade should be self lined. If you want to use lining on these valances, then lining amount equals yardage amount.

V124, V139 (SEE CHAPTER: FABRIC SHADES)

V125, V126, V127, V128, V140

PLAIN FABRIC WITH LINING

Finished length plus 10'' equals cut length. Pleat-to X's two and one half, divided by fabric width, rounded to next whole width equals widths required. Widths X's cut length divided by 36 equals yardage.

PLAIN FABRIC SELF LINED

Finished length X's two plus 10'' equals cut length. Pleat-to X's two and one half, divided by fabric width, rounded to next whole width. This equals widths required. Widths X's cut length divided by 36 equals yardage.

PRINTED FABRICS WITH LINING (lining recommended)

Finished length plus 10'' divided by repeat, then rounded to higher whole number (if number is fractional). Whole number X's repeat equals cut length. Pleat-to X's two and a half divided by fabric width, rounded to next whole width. Width X's cut length divided by 36 equals yardage.

ADDITIONAL INFORMATION

We have attempted to follow the industry standards with the above information. Your workroom may vary in cut lengths, and other requirements. Its best to check with your workroom to see if above formulas are acceptable.

Generally if you want to add lining to above valances then lining amount equals yardage amount.

Swag with Asymetric Cascades

Boxed Swag Valance

Swags Over Austrian Shade

Swag with Rosettes & Bow in Middle

TYPES OF SWAGS & CASCADES

Wrapped Swag

Open Swag

Gathered Swag

Pleated Swag

Standard Cascade

Stacked Cascade

Gathered Cascade

SWAGS & CASCADES
Yardage Requirements

Swag

Cascade

SWAG WIDTH, BOARD FACE & NIMBER OF SWAGS

Swags may vary in width from 20" to over 70". Very small swags will have only a few folds. Extremely wide swags will have a limited drop length. The width of the swag is determined by the board face and the number of swags that will be used on each treatment. The following guide will help determine the number of swags needed based on the board face. The guide is based on the assumption that swag overlap will start approximately 1/2 or less the width of the swag face.

IF BOARD FACE IS:	NUMBER OF SWAGS NEEDED IS:
36" to 48"	1 swag
49" to 70"	2 swags
71" to 100"	3 swags
101" to 125"	4 swags
126" to 150"	5 swags
151" to 175"	6 swags
176" to 200"	7 swags
201" to 225"	8 swags
226" to 250"	9 swags
251" to 275"	10 swags
276" to 300"	11 swags

SWAG WIDTH:
To find the width of each swag, divide the board face width by one or more than the number of swags used and multiply by 2.

Example:
Board face width = 127"   Number of swags = 5
127" ÷ 6 = 21.16 × 2 = 42.33 or 43" width for each swag.

The standard drop lengths of swags are 16", 18", or 20". Usually 6 or 7 folds are placed across the top of a traditional swag with a standard drop. Swags that have shallow drops of 12" will have 3 or 4 folds.

The chart below is an average guide to help you in finding swag drop based on face width.

Swags are top treatments or valances, used over draperies or blinds or sometimes alone. They are usually draped into soft, graceful folds, using fabrics that drape easily. It is more interesting to use an uneven number of swags. Swags should be lined.

Cascades are folded pieces of fabric that fall from the top of the drapery heading or valance to create a zig-zag effect. Cascades must be lined with the cover fabric or one that contrasts.

Yardage:
Swags — Based on an average of 44" per swag, you will need 2 yards of fabric per swag.

Cascades — Double the longest length, add 4" and multiply by 36. This will give you the number of yards needed for a single pair of cascades.

IF SWAG FACE WITH IS:	AVERAGE DROP WILL BE:
20"	10" to 13"
25"	12" to 17"
30"	14" to 19"
35"	14" to 20"
40"	14" to 21"
45"	16" to 23"
50"	16" to 23"
OVER 60"	18" to 24"

CASCADES & JABOTS

Double Cascade

Single Cascades

CASCADES

SINGLE TRADITIONAL CASCADE
(Yardage is for one cascade only)

Lined in contrasting fabric:
Length: *CL of face = FL (long point) plus 4" extra
CL of lining = FL (long point) plus 4 " extra
Width: Allow one width for face & one width for lining

Self lined:
Length: FL (long point) x 2 plus 4" = CL of face & lining
Width: One width will accomodate face & lining

DOUBLE CASCADE
Length: Contrast or self lined — FL plus 4" = CL
Width: (face) — one width per Double Cascade (up to 14")
(lining) — one width per Double Cascade

Note: *CL = cut length   FL = Finished Length

JABOTS

Jabots are decorative pieces of fabric that are hung over seams
or between swags on a valance. Jabots may be tie
shaped, cone shaped, or rounded on the bottom.

Yardage: Allow approximately one third yard of fabric for each jabot.

EMPIRE SWAG WITH JABOTS

Tie Jabot

Inverted Tie Jabot

Double Inverted Tie Jabot

Inverted Cone Jabot

Rounded Jabot

Cornice Box with Ruffle on Bottom

Cornice Box with Swag & Rosettes

Cornice Box with Shirred & Flat Panels

Shirred Cornice Box

Cornice Box with Pleated Fabric in Middle

Cornice Box with Shirred
Band & Ruffled Cascade

Shaped Cornice Box with
Vertical Side Drops

Bottom Banded Cornice Box
with Matching Draperies

Shirred Cornice
over Tie Backs

Pelmet with Welt Edge
over Roman Shade

Shirred Pelmet over
Pleated Drapery

Real Wood Cornice with Painted Leaf Design

Cornice with Real Wood Header

Straight Cornice with Stenciled Design

Cornice with In-and-out Swag

Cornice with Shaped & Raised Banding

Cornice with Honeycomb Pleating

Cornice with Diagonally Arched Pleating

Cornice with Unique Angled Top & Welting

Straight Cornice with Diagonal Welts
& Center Rosette

Cornice with Rounded Gathered Top
& Large Scalloped Bottom

The dramatic Accordian Look
is created by rows of Mini-pleats

Brass Grommets & Front Cording
give a Nautical Look to this Shade

A Flat, simple Roman Shade that
draws up into graceful Folds when
raised

A Cord at each edge gives
needed support to this
Bottom-up Shade

Distinctive Horizontal Pleating makes this
a very popular & versatile Roman Shade

Alternate Groups of Mini-pleats
with Single Panels gives this
blind a striking look all its own

Soft Overlapping Folds
create a Cascading Effect
in this Roman Shade

Alternating Large & Small Pleats
form a Repeating Pattern
on this Roman Shade

FSVAL1

This Valance has Soft
Folds & No Returns.

FSVAL2

For a more finished look, Soft
Folds wrap around the sides of
this Roman Valance

FS124

Soft Mini-fold Roman Shade

FSV121

Roman Shade with Valance
Overlapping

FS100

This very simple Roman Shade is
flat when down & draws up in
graceful folds when raised

Measuring Instructions

Inside Installation

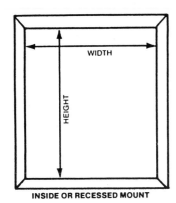

INSIDE OR RECESSED MOUNT

Outside Installation

OUTSIDE OR WALL MOUNT

A. Width: Measure width of window at the top, center and bottom of window, and use narrowest measurement when ordering. Specify on order form if inside clearance has been made. If no clearance has been allowed factory will deduct ¼" from overall width.

B. Length: Measure height of window from top of opening to top of sill, no allowance is made for length.

A. Width: Measure exact width of area to be covered. It is recommended that shades extend past actual window opening by 2" on each side. Furnish finished shade width, no allowances will be made.

B. Length: Measure length of area to be covered, allowing a minimum of 2½" at top of window to accomodate headerboard and brackets. (At this time you may want to take into consideration stackage of shades and allow for this in your length measurement.) Furnish finished shade length, no allowance will be made.

ALL INSTALLATIONS

A. Specify right or left cord position. If no cord position is indicated, cords will be corded to right hand side.

B. Specify cord length (length of cord needed for easy reach, when shade is completely down). If no specification is made, cord length will be approximately ⅓ length of shade.

C. For Pole Cloud, Cloud and Balloon shades, specify if length given is high or low point of pouff.

Square Footage Chart

SHADE LENGTH in inches	SHADE WIDTH in inches																				
	24	30	36	42	48	54	60	66	72	78	84	90	96	102	108	114	120	126	132	138	144
30	10	10	10	10	10	11¼	12½	13¾	15	16¼	17½	18¾	20	21¼	22½	23¾	25	26¼	27½	28¾	30
36	10	10	10	10½	12	13½	15	16½	18	19½	21	22½	24	25½	27	28½	30	31½	33	34½	36
42	10	10	10½	12¼	14	15¾	17½	19¼	21	22¾	24½	26¼	28	29¾	31½	33¼	35	36¾	38½	40¼	42
48	10	10	12	14	16	18	20	22	24	26	28	30	32	34	36	38	40	42	44	46	48
54	10	11¼	13½	15¾	18	20¼	22½	24¾	27	29¼	31½	33¾	36	38¼	40½	42¾	45	47¼	49½	51¾	54
60	10	12½	15	17½	20	22½	25	27½	30	32½	35	37½	40	42½	45	47½	50	52½	55	57½	60
66	11	13¾	16½	19¼	22	24¾	27½	30¼	33	35¾	38½	41¼	44	46¾	49½	52¼	55	57¾	60½	63¼	66
72	12	15	18	21	24	27	30	33	36	39	42	45	48	51	54	57	60	63	66	69	72
78	13	16¼	19½	22¾	26	29¼	32½	35¾	39	42¼	45½	48¾	52	55¼	58½	61¾	65	68¼	71½	74¾	78
84	14	17½	21	24½	28	31½	35	38½	42	45½	49	52½	56	59½	63	66½	70	73½	77	80½	84
90	15	18¾	22½	26¼	30	33¾	37½	41¼	45	48¾	52½	56¼	60	63¾	67½	71¼	75	78¾	82½	86¼	90
96	16	20	24	28	32	36	40	44	48	52	56	60	64	68	72	76	80	84	88	92	96
102	17	21¼	25½	29¾	34	38¼	42½	46¾	51	55¼	59½	63¾	68	72¼	76½	80¾	85	89¼	93½	97¾	102
108	18	22½	27	31½	36	40½	45	49½	54	58½	63	67½	72	76½	81	85½	90	94½	99	103½	108
114	19	23¾	28½	33¼	38	42¾	47½	52¼	57	61¾	66½	71¼	76	80¾	85½	90¼	95	99¾	104½	109¼	114
120	20	25	30	35	40	45	50	55	60	65	70	75	80	85	90	95	100	105	110	115	120
126	21	26¼	31½	36¾	42	47¼	52½	57¾	63	68¼	73½	78¾	84	89¼	94½	99¾	105	110¼	115½	120¾	126
132	22	27½	33	38½	44	49½	55	60½	66	71½	77	82½	88	93½	99	104½	110	115½	121	126½	132
138	23	28¾	34½	40¼	46	51¾	57½	63¼	69	74¾	80½	86¼	92	97¾	103½	109¼	115	120¾	126½	132¼	138
144	24	30	36	42	48	54	60	66	72	78	84	90	96	102	108	114	120	126	132	138	144

© 1986 Carol's Roman Shades

Yardage Requirements

FS100 • FS101 • FS104 • FS106 • FS107 • FS108
FS110 • FS111 • FS112 • FS121 • FSV124

1. **Width of Shade:**
   Measure width of area to be covered by shade. Figure how many widths of material across area you will need. When more than one width is needed, estimate full width only. One width will cover 4" less than actual, width of fabric.

2. **Length of Shade:**
   Measure length of area to be covered by shade and proceed below to appropriate design:
   FS106, FS111. Multiply length of shade by 1.25, and add 14" for top and bottom hems.
   FS108. Multiply lengths x 1.33 and add 14" for top and bottom hems.
   FS100. Multiply length by 1.5, and add 14" for top and bottom hems.
   FS104. Multiply length x 1.75, and add 14" for top and bottom hems.
   FS101, FS110. Multiply length by 2.0, and add 14" for top and bottom hems.
   FS107. Multiply length x 2.65, and add 14" for top and bottom hems.

3. **Multiply Widths x Lengths = Fabric Required in inches. Divide by 36" for yardage.***
   * **Important:** when working with a fabric that has a pattern repeat, add one repeat per width of fabric.

FS102 • FS102V • FS103 • FS109 • FS109V • FS113
FS117 • FS123 • FS125 • FSA126 • FSA127
(We suggest wrinkle resistant fabric)

1. **Width of Shade or Valance:**
   Measure width of area to be covered by shade or valance. Multiply by three. Divide this number by width of fabric, this equals number of widths required. When more than one width is required estimate full width only.

2. **Length of Shade or Valance:**
   Measure length of area to be covered by shade or valance.
   FS102, FS103, FS109, FS113: length of shade plus 36" for hem and fullness.

3. **Multiply Widths x Lengths = Fabric Required in inches. Divide by 36" for yardage.***
   * **Important:** when working with a fabric that has a pattern repeat, add one repeat per width of fabric.
   • **FS117.** Add ½ yard per linear foot for ruffle.
   • **FS109V, FS102V.** add 1 yard per 1½ linear foot for valance.

• FS115 •
(We suggest wrinkle resistant fabric)

1. **Width of Shade or Valance:**
   Measure width of area to be covered by shade or valance. Multiply x 1.65. Divide this number by width of fabric, this equals number of widths required. When more than one width is required estimate full width only.

2. **Length of Shade or Valance.**
   Measure length of area to be covered by shade or valance and proceed to appropriate design:
   FS115: length of shade x 3.

3. **Multiply Widths x Length = Fabric Required in Inches. Divide by 36" for yardage***
   *Important: when working with a fabric that has a pattern repeat, add 1 repeat per width of fabric.

Rod Top & Bottom Curtain with Ties
and Center Sleeve

Rod Pocket Curtain with Tie-backs
and Center Sleeve

Bow Tied Ruffled Tie-backs

Tab-top Curtains on Dec. Rod

Ruffled Tie-backs over Balloon Shade

Tab Top Curtains on Dec Rod

Curved Rod Pocket Valance
over Straight Curtains

Ruffled Tie-backs over Shutters

Lace Curtain & Valance
Threaded on Rod

Banded Tie-back Curtains

Banded Valance over Tie-backs

Tab Top Banded Curtains Tied Back

Tiered Curtains with Ribbon Banding

Sheer Lace Tied-back Curtains
with Gathered Valance

Shirred Cafe Curtain on High Rod

Cafe Curtains with French Pleated
Tops on Rings

Scalloped Valance over
Cafe Curtains

Priscilla Curtains with Ruffles

Valance on Brass Dec. Rod over Tied
back Curtains with Ruffles

Rod-Top Curtains with High Ties
and Large Ruffles

Priscilla Curtains with Rod Pocket Top

Cafe Curtains with Arched Top & Valance

Cafe Curtains on Brass Rod with Gathered Valance

Traditional Swag with Mini-blind

Pleated Tab-top Cafe Curtains on Brass Rod

Cafe Curtains Shirred top-to-bottom
between Two Rods

Tied-back Curtains Gathered on Rod

Drapery Gathered on a Dec. Rod &
Tied Back with Large Bows

Austrian Shade with Ruffles

Double Cafe Curtains with Scalloped
Top on Brass Rod

Tab-tied Curtains on Brass Dec. Rod

French Pleated Curtains with Scalloped
Heading on Brass Dec. Rod

Arched Valance

Valance with Bows

Alternate — Traditional Swag

Rod Pocket Valance with
Cathedral Top

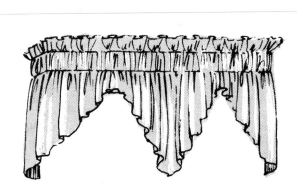

Double Arched Rod Pocket Valance

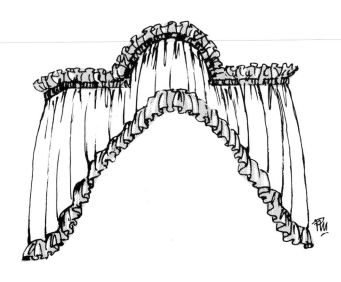

Cathedral Top Valance with tapered sides

**STRAIGHT PLAIN
STYLE No. 1**

**TAPERED PLAIN
STYLE No. 2**

**STRAIGHT WITH BANDING
STYLE No. 3**

**TAPERED WITH WELT CORD
STYLE No. 4**

**SHIRRED JUMBO WELT CORD
STYLE No. 5**

**STRAIGHT SHIRRED
WITH WELT CORD
STYLE No. 6**

**STRAIGHT SHIRRED
STYLE No. 7**

**BRAIDED
STYLE No. 8**

**STRAIGHT WITH ROSETTE
STYLE No. 9**

ACCESSORIES

Placemats

Seat Cushions

Lamp Shades

Napkins & Napkin Rings

Rosettes

Bows

Sunburst

Hourglass–Rod Top & Bottom

Diamond–Rod Top & Bottom

Hourglass Rod Top & Bottom

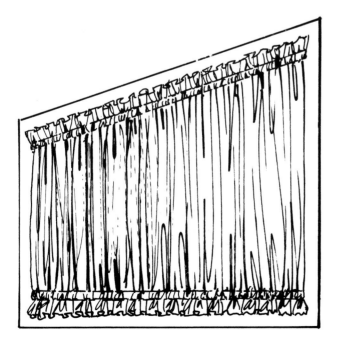

Slant Rod Top & Bottom

YARDAGE AMOUNTS

PILLOWS
YARDAGE AMOUNTS FOR ONE PILLOW:
(45" – 54" fabric)

	12" – 15"	16" – 18"	20" – 24"
KNIFE EDGE PILLOW, ETC.	1/2 yd	3/4 yd	1 yd
OPTIONS			
1/4" welt	1/4 yd	1/4 yd	1/4 yd
1" welt	1/2 yd	1/2 yd	3/4 yd
3" – 4" ruffle (54" fabric)	1 yd	1 yd	1 1/2 yd

CHAIR CUSHIONS:
(45" – 54" fabric)

	16" or smaller
Body of cushion	1/2 yd
1/4 welt & ties	1/2 yd
Ruffle (up to 3")	1 yd

DIRECTOR CHAIR COVER
1 yd

BOLSTERS:

	36"	45"	54"
36"	1 1/2 yds	1 1/2 yds	1 yd
39"	2 yds	1 1/2 yds	1 yd
60"	2 yds	2 yds	2 yds
72"	2 1/2 yds	2 yds	2 yds

TABLESKIRTS:
Yardage amounts — If total diameter of skirt is greater than width of fabric, the length of fabric needed is double the diameter of skirt. If total diameter of skirt is as much or less than width of fabric, the length of fabric is needed is one diameter measurement of skirt.

******ADD 1 REPEAT OF PATTERN FOR PRINTED FABRICS******

Half-round Box Pleated Valance
with Draped Fabric held by Rosettes
Upholstered Headboard with Throw Spread

Fabric Draped over Decorative Pole
Coverlet with Tailored Dust Ruffle

Half-round Ruffled Valance with
Fabric Draped over Hold Backs
Upholstered Headboard with Throw Spread

Rod Pocket Valance with Ruffled Tie-backs
Upholstered Headboard & Throw Spread

DUST RUFFLES

Tailored

Shirred

Box Pleated

HOW TO MEASURE:
(Exact measurements are necessary)
A — Length of Boxsprings
B — Width of Boxsprings
C — Drop from top of Boxsprings to floor

UPHOLSTERED HEADBOARDS

STYLE #1

STYLE #4

STYLE #5

STYLE #7

STYLE #6

STYLE #2

STYLE #3

DIMENSIONS

STYLE	TWIN	FULL	QUEEN	KING
1,2,5,7	41W X 51H	56W X 53H	62W X 55H	81W X 56H
3	41W X 53H	56W X 55H	62W X 57H	81W X 57H
4,6	41W X 49H	56W X 49H	62W X 51H	81W X 53H

UPHOLSTERED BENCHES

Plain Covered Bench

Curved Scalloped Bench

Double Bench with
Shirred Skirt

Plain Bench with
Upholstered Legs & Top

PILLOW SHAMS

Sham with 3" Ruffle

Plain Sham with
1/4" Welt

Quilted Sham with
2 1/2" Flange

Plain Sham with
Double Ruffle

Sham with 1/4" Welt
and Ruffle

Double Ruffled Sham
with 1/2" Welt

Cylindrical Bolster
with Welt Trim

Wedge Bolster with
Welt Trim

Rectangular Bolster
with Welt Trim

BOW KNOT

LEAF

CLOVER

BOW KNOT

STRAIGHT DIAMOND

FLORENTINE

POPPY

SHELL

BAMBOO

CHINESE

CHEVRON

DIAGONAL

PAGODA

SCROLL

VINE

HERITAGE

VERMICILLI

ZIGZAG SQUARE

CLOUDS

LA PLUME

ZIGZAG DIAMOND

OUTLINE QUILT

BUTTERFLY

CHANNEL

Yardage Schedule

BOLSTERS

	36"	45"	54"
Twin	36"	1 1/2 yards	1 1/2 yards	1 yard
Full	39"	2 yards	1 1/2 yards	1 yard
Queen	60"	2 yards	2 yards	2 yards
King	72"	2 1/2 yards	2 yards	2 yard

Add 1 Repeat of Pattern For Prints.

SPREADS

	36"	48"	54"
Twin	12 yards	8 yards	8 yards
Full	12 yards	12 yard	8 yards
Queen	15 yards	12 yards	12 yards
King	15 yards	12 yards	12 yards

Additional Yardage Requirements: For Prints—Add 1 yard
Additional Yardage Optional Features
For Reverse Sham—Add 3 yards   For Jumbo Cord—Add 2 yards

PILLOW SHAMS

1 1/2 yards—Ruffles add 1 1/2 yards

COMFORTER YARDAGE

Twin, Full, Queen—7 yds./side
King—11 yds./side

DUSTERS

45" or Wider

	Tailored	Shirred or 4" Box Pleat
Twin	2 3/4 yards	6 1/2 yards
Full	2 3/4 yards	7 yards
Queen	3 yards	7 1/2 yards
King	3 yards	7 1/2 yards

36" Fabric

	Tailored	Shirred or 4" Box Pleat
Twin	3 3/4 yards	8 1/2 yards
Full	3 3/4 yards	8 1/2 yards
Queen	4 1/2 yards	10 yards
King	4 1/2 yards	10 yards

GENERAL INFORMATION

STANDARD DROPS

Bedspreads 21"
Coverlets 12"
Dusters 14"
Pillow Tuck 15"
Drop over 22" Add:

Bedspreads are made to fit following standard bed sizes.

Twin   39 x 75
Full   54 x 75
Queen   60 x 80
King   72 x 84
Round Bedspreads 7', 8' (Made to your measurements)

Ruffled Swags Over Cafe Shutters

Two-tone Swag Over Full Shutters

Shutter With Shirred Fabric Insert

Gathered Valance Over Louvered Shutters

**Cornice Box Over White Wood
Blinds With Wide Tapes**

Sunburst Shutter Over French Door Shutters

Leaded Glass Over Wide Blade Shutters

**1'' Wood Blind in Natural Finish
With Cloud Valance**

Cathedral Window with
Custom Fitted Shutters

Shutters Custom Fitted to
Slanted Clerestory Window

French Doors with Wood
Blinds & Chevron Valances

Traditional Shutters
on Tall Window

Balloon Valance
over Wood Blind

Bishop Sleeve Draperies
over Wood Blind

Fabric Swag with Side Drop
over Wood Blind

Box Pleated Valance
over Wood Blind

Fabric Draped in Double
Swag

over Wood Blind

Arched Gathered Valance
over Wood Venetian Blind

Tabbed Valance on Dec Rod
over Wood Blind

Swags & Jabots
over Half Shutters

Shirred Valance with Ruffle over
Gathered Side Draperies & Wood Blind

Bishop Sleeve Arched Valance
over Plantation Shutters

Cloud Valance over Half Shutters

**Tab Curtains Tied Back
Over Roller Shade**

Flat Panels Pulled Back Over Pleated Shades

**Puffed and Ruffled Valance
Over Pleated Shade**

**Gathered Swag and Cascade
Over Pleated Shade**

Cloud Valance Over Mini Blind

Alternate Valance Styles

**Pleated Shade With Arched
Pleated Shade At Top**

Unique Geometric Valance Over Mini Blind

Lace Tie Backs on Dec Rod
over Mini Blind

Box Pleated Valance
over Pleated Shade

Scalloped Awning Valance
over Mini Blind

Full Gathered Valance
on Double Rods

**Handkerchief Tie
over Pleated Blind**

**Swag with Tassles
& Fringe**

**Cloud Shade with
Ruffled Top & Tassles**

Short Swag on Dec Rod

Multiple Lace Fabric Swags on Dec Rod

Simple Shirred Cornice Over Vertical Blinds

Fabric or Wallpaper Inserts
Add a Designer Touch to Verticals

Double Gathered Cornice Over Vertical Blinds

Vertical Blinds With Stagecoach Valance

Slant-top Vertical Blinds

Vertical Blinds With Cornice Top

Verticals Are A Great Solution To Bay Windows

Shirred Cloud Valance Adds
Softness to Vertical Blinds

Slanted Windows
with Vertical Blinds

Scalloped Pleated Valance
over Vertical Blinds

Double Brass Rods over Vertical Blinds
with Brass Trim at Bottom

Decorative Stencil Design
on Vertical Blinds

Swag with Ruffled Side Drops
over Vertical Blinds

Floor Length Fabric Swagged on
Shirred Rod over Vertical Blinds

Bay Window with Bishop Sleeve
Effect over Vertical Blinds

Draperies Folded and Gathered Over Sheers

This Popular European Design Adds Elegance

Another Unique European Style Valance

Kingston Valance With Ruffles and Border Top

Fabric Swagged Over Pole
With Cord and Tassle Trim

Two Large and One Small Swag
With Cascades

Arched Ruffled Sunburst and Tie Backs
Over Cafe Curtains

Deep Swag and Full Tie Backs are a
Popular European Style

Swagged Fabric with Cord Trim
over Asymetric Tie Back

Gathered Draperies Pulled
Back to Show Lining

Special Swag & Jabot Effect

Fabric Swagged through
Large brass Rings

Asymetric Swag held
by Fabric Ties

Handkerchief Valance over
Asymetric Tie Back

Fabric Loosely Tied to
Covered Dec Rod

Draperies over Bay Window with
Large Swags held by Bows